CONTENTS

SIGNS OF THE SEASONS
4

SPRING
10

SUMMER
14

AUTUMN
18

WINTER
22

PEOPLE AND THE SEASONS
26

GLOSSARY
30

FURTHER INFORMATION
31

INDEX
32

SIGNS OF THE SEASONS

Have you noticed how certain things happen at a particular time of year? Birds lay their eggs in spring. Butterflies appear in summer. In autumn the leaves on some trees turn yellow and gold and fall to the ground. In winter it turns colder and snow may fall.

DISCOVERING GEOGRAPHY

SEASONS

Rebecca Hunter

www.raintreepublishers.co.uk
Visit our website to find out more information about **Raintree** books.

To order:
 Phone 44 (0) 1865 888112
 Send a fax to 44 (0) 1865 314091
Visit the Raintree Bookshop at **www.raintreepublishers.co.uk** to browse our catalogue and order online.

First published in Great Britain by Raintree,
Halley Court, Jordan Hill, Oxford
OX2 8EJ, part of Harcourt Education.

Raintree is a registered trademark of Harcourt
Education Ltd.

© Harcourt Education Ltd 2003
First published in paperback in 2004
The moral right of the proprietor has been asserted.

Produced for Raintree by Discovery Books Ltd
Design: Ian Winton
Editorial: Rebecca Hunter
Consultant: Jeremy Bloomfield
Commissioned photography: Chris Fairclough
Illustrations: Keith Williams, Stefan Chabluk and
Pamela Goodchild
Production: Jonathan Smith

Originated by Dot Gradations Ltd
Printed and bound in China by South China
Printing Company

ISBN 1 844 21680 2 (hardback)
07 06 05 04 03
10 9 8 7 6 5 4 3 2 1

ISBN 1 844 21685 3 (paperback)
08 07 06 05 04
10 9 8 7 6 5 4 3 2 1

British Library Cataloguing in Publication Data
Hunter, Rebecca
Seasons. – (Discovering Geography)
508.2
A full catalogue record for this book is available from the
British Library.

Acknowledgements
The publishers would like to thank the following for
permission to reproduce photographs:
Bruce Coleman pp. **4**, **5** top (Kim Taylor), **5** bottom, **14**
(Tore Hagman), **16** (Kim Taylor), **17** top, **17** bottom
(Stephen J. Krasemann), **20**, **21** (Gordon Langsbury), **23**
top (Jane Burton), **23** bottom (Stephen J. Krasemann);
Chris Fairclough pp. **10** inset, **22**; Getty Images pp. **8**, **9**
(Arnulf Husmo), **12** top (G. Bumgarner), **18** top, (R.K.G.
Photography), **26** (Donna Day), **27** top (Andy Sacks), **27**
bottom (Jess Stock), **28** bottom, (Bruce Forster), **29** (John
& Eliza Forder); Oxford Scientific Films pp. **12** bottom
(John Gerlach), **18** bottom (Terry Andrewartha), **20**
bottom (Jim Clare), **28** top (David Curl); Papilio
Photographic p. **25**.

Cover photograph of leaves reproduced with permission
of Bruce Coleman.

The publishers would like to thank the following schools
for their help in providing equipment, models and
locations for photography sessions: Bedstone College,
Bucknell, Moor Park, Ludlow and Packwood Haugh,
Shrewsbury.

Every effort has been made to contact copyright holders
of any material reproduced in this book.
Any omissions will be rectified in subsequent printings if
notice is given to the publishers.

Any words appearing in the text in bold, **like
this**, are explained in the Glossary.

All these events are signs of different seasons. A season is a time of year that has a particular kind of weather. The changes in the seasons affect all types of plants and animals, and humans too.

▲ *A blue tit feeds its young in spring or early summer.*

▶ *It is fun walking to school in summer when the weather is warm and sunny.*

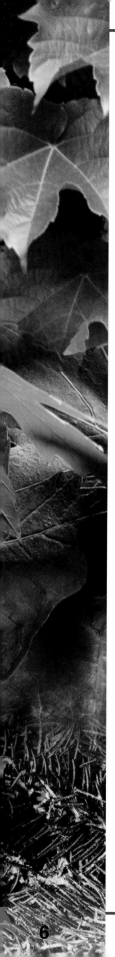

REASONS FOR SEASONS

Seasons are caused by the way Earth moves around, or orbits, the Sun. It takes 365 days and 6 hours for Earth to orbit the Sun. Because of the way Earth is tilted, one half gets more sunlight than the other for half the year. When the northern **hemisphere** is tilted towards the Sun, it will have long, sunny days. The countries there will be having summer.

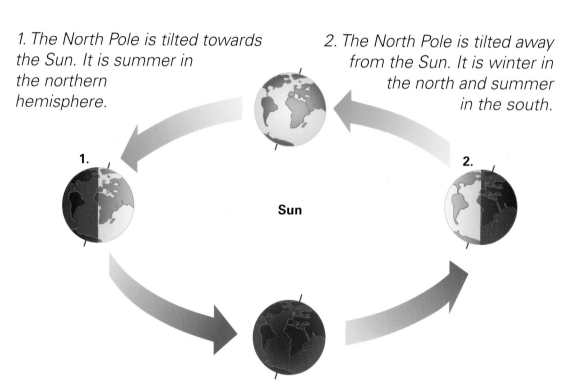

1. The North Pole is tilted towards the Sun. It is summer in the northern hemisphere.

2. The North Pole is tilted away from the Sun. It is winter in the north and summer in the south.

Sun

At the same time, the southern hemisphere will be having short winter days because it is tilted away from the Sun. Six months later, when Earth is on the other side of the Sun, the seasons will have swapped.
It will be summer in the south and winter in the north. In between summer and winter, the hemispheres will have autumn or spring.

The seasons are very different in different parts of the world. When you look at a map of the world, you will see an imaginary line in the middle called the **equator**. To the north and south of the equator are two more imaginary lines called the tropic of Cancer and the tropic of Capricorn.

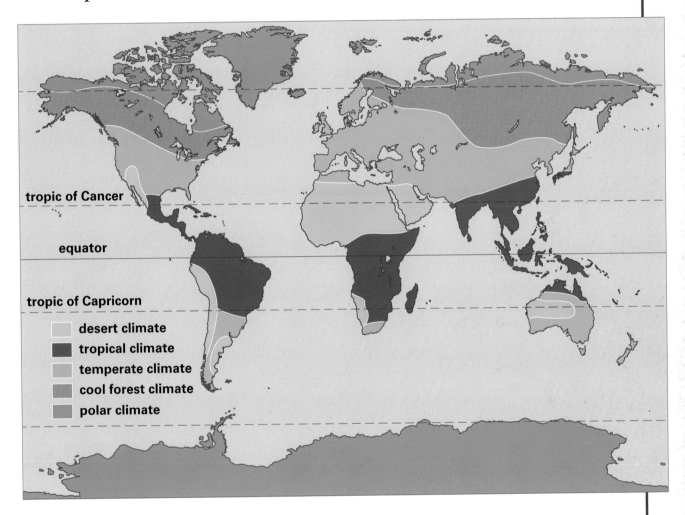

tropic of Cancer

equator

tropic of Capricorn

desert climate
tropical climate
temperate climate
cool forest climate
polar climate

The area between these two lines is known as the **tropics**. The weather here is always hot. At the far north and south of Earth are the polar regions. Polar **climates** are cold and dry. The area between the tropics and the polar regions is called the temperate zone. Temperate regions have warm summers and cold winters.

TROPICAL SEASONS

Because of the shape of Earth, the land in the **tropics** gets more sunlight than the land at the Poles where the Sun's rays are spread over a wider area.

North Pole

Sun's rays   the tropics

South Pole

Countries in the tropics have hot or warm weather all year. The seasons differ in rainfall. Seasons in the tropics are either wet or dry.

POLAR SEASONS

The Poles have only two seasons. Six months of summer and six months of winter. Polar seasons are **extreme**. In winter at the South Pole, the Sun does not rise at all for several months. At the same time it is summer at the North Pole. In parts of Finland in northern Europe, there is daylight for 24 hours a day in summer. Because of this, polar areas are called the 'lands of the midnight Sun'.

TEMPERATE SEASONS

Between the Poles and the tropics are the temperate zones. There are four different seasons: spring, summer, autumn and winter. The further away from the **equator** you go, the more obvious the seasons become. Sweden has much colder winters than Greece, where it remains warm all winter.

This picture shows the movement of the Sun throughout one day in northern Norway in the middle of summer. Over 24 hours the Sun does not set at all.

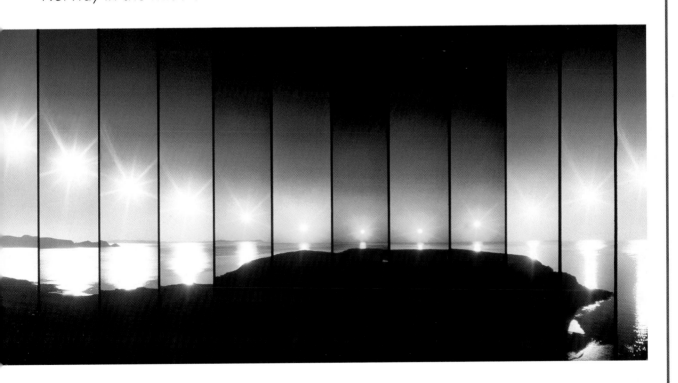

SPRING

In spring the days begin to get longer and the weather starts to get warmer. After the short, cold winter days, everyone enjoys seeing the sunshine again and the animals and plants start to wake up and grow.

SPRING GROWTH

Many plants stop growing in winter. Spring is the time everything starts to grow again. Root tips grow longer and push their way through the soil. Buds on the trees get ready to burst into new green leaves.

Seeds, left behind from the year before, start to grow, and spring flowers shoot up from bulbs. The bulb is a store of food that helps the plant grow until its leaves appear.

Daffodils are spring flowers that grow from bulbs.

PROJECT

Grow your own seedlings.

You will need:
sunflower seeds
a small watering can
a notebook and pencil
a few pots
compost
water
a tape measure or a ruler.

1. Fill each pot with compost.

2. Plant a few seeds in each pot and water them. Leave the pots in a sunny position.

3. Water the pots every day and check for signs of growth.

4. When the seeds start to grow you can measure them each day.

5. Keep a record of their growth.

ANIMALS IN SPRING

For many animals winter is a hard time with cold **temperatures** and little food. In spring the temperatures are warmer, and life becomes easier.

A tiger swallowtail butterfly on some oxeye daisies.

The growth of new plants means there is more food available for animals. Bees, beetles and butterflies are some of the insects that eat more of this food and start to **breed** in spring.

Other animals eat insects. Many birds **migrate**, or move to another region or **climate**, to escape the winter weather. They return for the summer to feed on the new supply of insects. The European swallow spends the winter 11,000 kilometres (7000 miles) away in South Africa.

In spring birds begin to make their nests. Sometimes they choose unusual spots for nests.

This great grey owl is nesting on a tree stump.

PROJECT

Raise your own butterflies.

You will need:
*a large jar with holes in the lid
some butterfly caterpillars
tissue paper.*

1. Check the leaves of plants, bushes and trees for caterpillars. Oak trees and cabbage leaves are good places to look.

! Don't touch caterpillars; some can give you a bad rash.

2. Gently shake your caterpillars off the leaves into the jar with a layer of damp tissue paper in the bottom. Keep this paper damp, but not wet.

3. Make sure you collect leaves from the plant you found these insects on. Use these leaves to feed the caterpillars. If you don't feed them the right food, they will die.

4. When each caterpillar is fully grown, it attaches itself to a twig. Then its skin hardens into a pupa. It will stay like this for several weeks until the caterpillar has changed into a butterfly.

5. In the end, the pupa case will split, and the adult butterfly will crawl out.

6. You will be able to find out what kind of butterfly it is. Look it up in a book on butterflies. Then let it fly away.

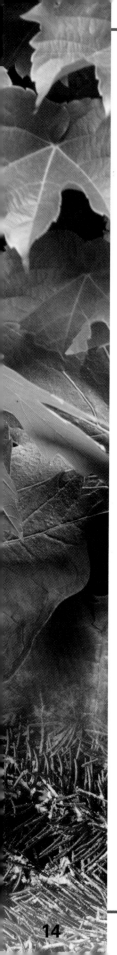

SUMMER

Summer is the hottest season of the year. The Sun rises earlier and sets later in summer, so the days are long and warm. Plants grow fast and the whole countryside seems to turn green.

PHOTOSYNTHESIS

light energy from the Sun

plant growth

water is taken in from the roots

PHOTOSYNTHESIS

Green plants need sunlight to grow. Their green leaves capture the energy in sunlight and turn it into sugars. The plant uses the sugars for growth. This process is called **photosynthesis**.

Water moves through a plant all the time. It is taken in by the roots and passes out again through the leaves. You can prove this by doing an experiment.

PROJECT

Collecting water from plants.

You will need:
a leafy tree or shrub
two large plastic bags
some string.

1. On a dry day, tie a plastic bag over some leaves on a tree or shrub. If you can find a twig with no leaves on it, tie another bag over this as well.

2. Come back after a few hours. The bag over the leaves should have collected some moisture in it. The other bag will be dry.

3. You have collected the water from just a few leaves. Imagine how much water a whole forest of trees would give off.

TREE-MENDOUS!

An average-sized tree will take as much as 50 buckets of water out of the ground on a hot day.

FLOWERS

As well as producing green leaves, many plants flower in summer. Flowers produce the seeds of a plant, but first they also need **pollen**. Pollination takes place when pollen from one flower is taken to another flower of the same kind. Insects, such as bees and butterflies, and some birds help by carrying pollen from one flower to another. They are attracted to the flowers by their bright colours and sweet scents.

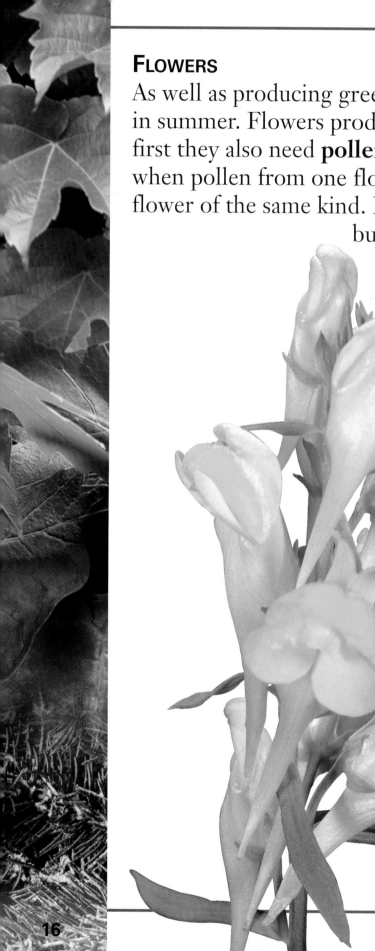

A bee collecting nectar from a common toadflax flower.

Summer is the time when there is a good food supply for animals. They make use of the extra food to fatten themselves and to feed their young.

CHANGING COLOURS

Some animals change colour with the seasons. The Arctic hare and Arctic fox have white fur in winter to keep them well hidden in the snow. When summer comes, and the snow melts, they shed their coats. They grow a new summer coat to match the soil and shrubs.

▼ *An Arctic fox in its winter coat.*

AUTUMN

One of the first signs of autumn is that the leaves on the trees turn yellow, orange or brown and fall to the ground. In autumn the days get cooler and shorter, and plants and animals sense that winter is coming.

▶ *Colourful autumn forests in the Wasatch Mountains in Utah, USA.*

SEEDS

Autumn is the time for plants to shed their seeds. Seeds are spread around in different ways. Some seeds are inside a covering called a fruit. Some fruits, such as berries, are soft and juicy and good to eat. Birds and animals eat the fruit, spreading the seeds around in their droppings.

Some trees, such as the ash, box elder and sycamore have seeds with wings. The wind makes these seeds fly like helicopters, carrying them far away.

PROJECT

Flying seeds.

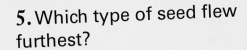

You will need:
a collection of different kinds of seeds with wings
a chair or set of steps
a tape measure
a friend to help.

1. Take your seeds into your garden or a park.

2. Stand on the chair or steps and throw the seeds into the air, one type at a time.

3. Notice how the seeds fly and how far.

4. Measure the distance each seed falls and record it on a chart like the one below.

5. Which type of seed flew furthest?

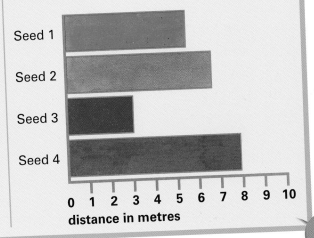

Seed 1
Seed 2
Seed 3
Seed 4

0 1 2 3 4 5 6 7 8 9 10
distance in metres

Evergreen trees have fruits called cones. It takes two years for most cones to grow fully and for their seeds to ripen. The cones will only open and shed their seeds in dry weather. If you find a closed cone on the ground, bring it inside and put it in a warm place. In time it will open, and you will see the seeds inside.

PREPARING FOR WINTER

In autumn, animals start to get ready for winter. Most animals need to find ways to store food for the cold months ahead. All summer they have been getting ready for winter by eating well and storing extra fat in their bodies.

Some animals and birds collect and hide food. Squirrels race around in autumn hiding nuts. They will not remember where they have hidden them all. So without knowing it, they have helped plant many new trees.

The acorn woodpecker pecks holes in a tree to store acorns.

MIGRATION AND HIBERNATION

Animals that cannot survive in the cold have two choices. They can either **migrate** to warmer areas, or **hibernate** to avoid the cold weather. Birds find it easier to migrate and the distances they travel can be huge. The Arctic tern (below) travels 40,000 kilometres, (24,800 miles) from the Arctic to the Antarctic each year.

Hibernating animals slow down their body processes, so that the body is only just alive. True hibernators remain inactive all winter, because they would lose too much energy if they woke up.

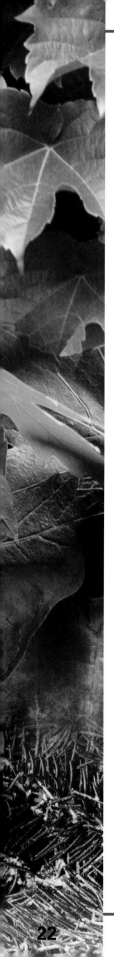

WINTER

Everything seems to slow down in winter. The days get shorter and the **temperatures** fall. Plants stop growing. Many trees look dead without their leaves.

Winter weather is much colder. If the temperatures drop below freezing, frosts may occur in the early mornings. Snow and sleet may fall. Ice and freezing rain are part of winter, too.

STAYING WARM

Many birds and other animals disappear from the countryside when they either **migrate** or go into **hibernation**. Small animals, such as squirrels and dormice, look for piles of leaves and stalks to hibernate in. As the plant life slowly breaks down, it gives off heat. This heat keeps the temperature from dropping below freezing. So the animals stay warm.

A dormouse hibernates in a nest of dry grass.

The animals that remain active in winter have to find ways of keeping themselves warm. Thick fur is essential to animals that are going to live through a cold winter.

A fox has a thick coat that keeps it warm in winter snow.

FINDING FOOD

Wild animals find it difficult to get enough food in winter. Plants are not growing and the ground may be covered with snow.

You can help the birds in your area live through winter by giving them food and, in some places, water. Do not start this project unless you are prepared to do it all winter because the birds will depend on you. They may suffer if you suddenly stop feeding them.

PROJECT

Make a bird feeder.

You will need:

an empty plastic bottle
a large bag of shelled, unsalted peanuts
some strong string
a few sticks of wood
a sharp knife or pair of scissors.

1. Ask an adult to help you cut some slits in the bottle. The slits should start in the middle and run to the top or bottom.

2. Push the sticks through the slits, so the birds will have something to perch on.

3. Fill the bottle with nuts and put the top on.

4. Hang the bottle from a strong branch.

5. Keep the bottle well filled. You could keep a chart of which birds come to visit the feeder. Draw each bird. A reference book will help you identify them.

Finding water is often difficult for animals and birds in winter, when streams and ponds may be frozen. A bird bath can help them out.

Water birds, such as these geese, can find it hard to get water when ponds and lakes are frozen.

PROJECT

Make a bird bath.

You will need:
a dustbin lid
some large stones
some water
a watering can.

1. Chose a place out in the open for the bird bath. The birds must be able to see if there are cats close by.

2. Use the stones to support the dustbin lid and make it level.

3. Fill the lid with water.

4. Check the bath every day. Fill it with clean water, and remove any ice that forms.

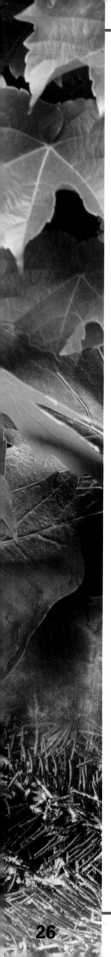

PEOPLE AND THE SEASONS

You may not realize it, but the seasons affect us every day of our lives. Just think about the clothes you wear and the food you eat. In summer you only need a few, light clothes. You drink lots of cold drinks and eat more salads and ice cream. As the weather gets colder in autumn, you need to wear more clothes. You want to eat hot food that warms you up.

It can be fun to play in autumn leaves.

Our behaviour also changes with the seasons. We spend much more time outside in the spring and summer months. We can play outdoor games and enjoy being out in the garden, countryside or parks.

We often go on holiday to places when the seasons are at their hottest or coldest. In summer, many people go to lakes or the seaside to cool off.

People go to places that have heavy snowfall in winter for skiing.

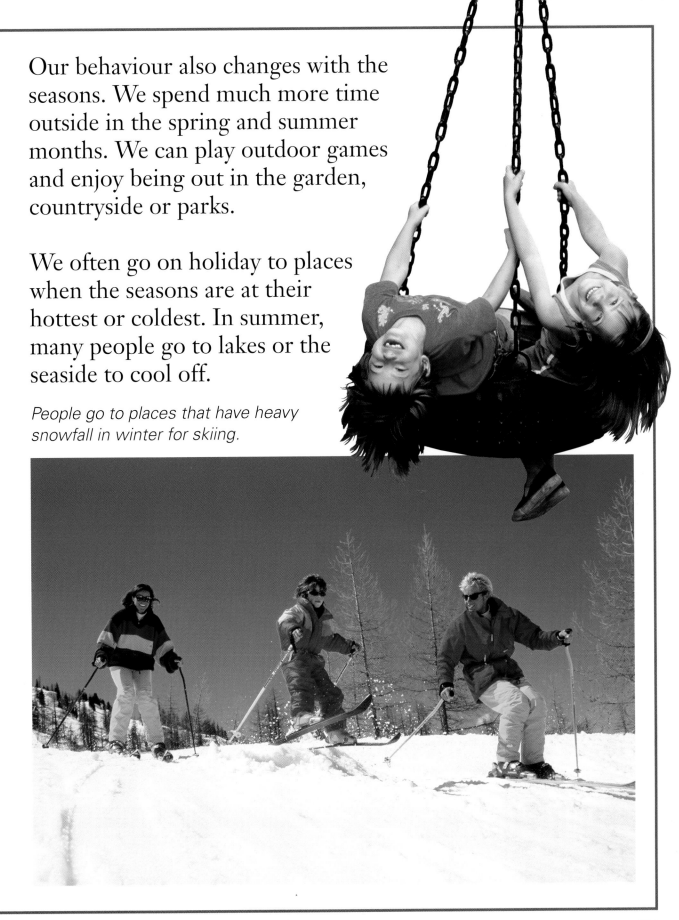

FARMING

Each season brings changes that affect the daily life and work of the farmer.

Farmers who grow crops have to get the land ready for planting in the winter. Autumn is when the fields are usually **ploughed**.

Seeds are sown in autumn or spring. Throughout the summer the crops have to be watered and sprayed against pests. The crops will be fully grown and ripe by the end of the summer. Now is the time to harvest them. It is important to get the harvest in before the weather turns bad. Heavy rains can flatten crops and ruin **hay**.

Farmers harvesting rye in Oregon, USA.

On farms that raise animals, different events happen at different times of year. Just as in the wild, young animals are usually born in the spring. The weather is warmer and the baby animals have a better chance of survival.

Sheep and cows spend the summer months grazing. Some will be taken to market at the end of the summer.

These sheep are able to survive winters outside. Their woolly coats keep them warm.

GLOSSARY

breed joining together of males and females to produce offspring or young

climate usual weather of a place from year to year

equator imaginary line around the middle of Earth. The equator is halfway between the North and South Poles.

evergreen plants that do not lose their leaves in winter

extreme very great or severe

hay dried grass that is fed to animals

hemisphere Earth can be divided into two hemispheres, one north of and one south of the equator

hibernation sleep-like state that some animals go into during winter

migration movement of animals to find food or warmth as the seasons change

photosynthesis method by which plants make food using water, carbon dioxide and sunlight

plough turn up soil to plant seeds

pollen fine powder produced by the male parts of a flowering plant

temperature how hot or cold something is

tropics area around the equator, between the tropic of Cancer and the tropic of Capricorn

FURTHER INFORMATION

BOOKS

The Greenwich Guide to the Seasons, Graham Dolan
(Heinemann Library, 2001)

Let's Explore: Changing Seasons, Henry Pluckrose
(Franklin Watts, 2000)

Our World: Seasons, Neil Morris (Belitha Press, 2002)

WEBSITES

BrainPOP – Seasons – learn all about the four seasons by watching the animated cartoon, doing the quiz, or trying the activity page.
http://www.brainpop.com/science/weather/seasons/index.weml

The Natural History Museum Wildlife Garden Seasons – take a look at the daily photographic record of the changing seasons over one year at the Natural History Museum's Wildlife Garden.
http://flood.nhm.ac.uk/cgi-bin/wgarden

What is weather? – learn about the weather, from wind direction to sunshine, and how this affects people all over the world.
http://www.bbc.co.uk/schools/whatisweather

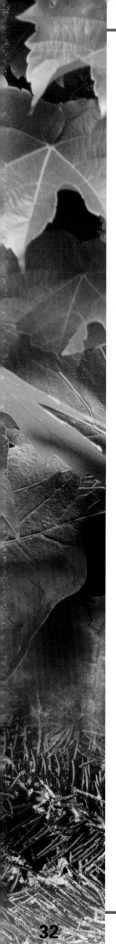

INDEX

animals 5, 10, 12, 17, 18, 20, 24
autumn 4, 6, 18, 19, 20, 21

berries 18
bird bath 25
bird feeder 24
birds 4, 12, 16, 18, 20, 21, 24, 25
buds 10
bulbs 10
butterflies 4, 12, 13, 16

climate 7, 12
cones 19
crops 28

Earth 6, 8
equator 7, 9

farm animals 29
farming 28, 29
fat 20
flowers 16
food 12, 17, 20
freezing rain 22
frosts 22
fruits 18
fur 17, 23

grazing 29

harvest 28
hibernation 21, 23
holidays 27

ice 22
insects 12, 16

leaves 4, 10, 14, 15, 16, 18, 22

midnight Sun 9
migration 21

nests 12
North Pole 6
nuts 20

people 5, 26, 27, 28
photosynthesis 14
planting 11, 28
plants 10, 12, 14, 15, 18
pollen 16

rain 8, 28

seeds 10, 11, 18, 19
skiing 27
sleet 22
snow 4, 17, 22, 24
South Pole 9
spring 6, 10, 11, 12, 13
squirrels 20
summer 6, 7, 9, 14, 15, 16, 17
Sun 6, 9, 14

temperate zones 7, 9
temperatures 12, 22, 23
trees 10, 15, 22
tropics 7, 8, 9

water 15, 24, 25
weather 5, 7, 8, 10, 26
winter 4, 6, 7, 9, 18, 20, 21, 22, 23